Conflict Resolution

by Robin Doak

Raintree

Chicago, Illinois

© 2004 Raintree

Published by Raintree, a division of Reed Elsevier, Inc.
Chicago, Illinois
Customer Service 888-363-4266
Visit our website at www.raintreelibrary.com

For information, address the publisher: Raintree, 100 N. LaSalle, Suite 1200, Chicago, IL 60602

Printed and bound in China.

08 07 06 05 04

10 9 8 7 6 5 4 3 2 1

Library of Congress Cataloging-in-Publication Data

Doak, Robin S. (Robin Santos), 1963–
    Conflict resolution / Robin Doak.
        p. cm. — (Character education)
Includes bibliographical references and index.
Contents: Resolving conflicts — The key is keeping calm — Respecting differences — Points of view — Keys to communication — Champions of non-violence — Dealing with bullies — Keeping schools peaceful — Apologizing and forgiving others — Fairness and conflict resolution — You and conflict resolution — Careers in conflict resolution — Working for world peace.
    ISBN 0-7398-7004-1 (lib. bdg.) — ISBN 1-4109-0322-2 (pbk.)
    1. Conflict management — Juvenile literature. [1. Conflict management.] I. Title. II. Series: Character education (Raintree (Firm))

    HM1126.D63 2004
    303.6'9 — dc21

                                                                                                2003005666

A Creative Media Applications, Inc. Production
WRITER: Robin Doak
DESIGN AND PRODUCTION: Alan Barnett, Inc.
EDITOR: Susan Madoff
COPYEDITOR: Laurie Lieb

PHOTO CREDITS:
Cover: © Royalty-Free/CORBIS
© Norbert Schaefer/CORBIS *page:* 5
AP/Wide World Photographs *pages:* 7, 8, 10, 11, 13, 14, 15, 18, 19, 20, 21, 22, 23, 28
© Ariel Skelley/CORBIS *page:* 9
© Jennie Woodcock; Reflections Photolibrary/CORBIS *page:* 17
© Stewart Cohen/Getty Images *page:* 25
© Bob Rowan; Progressive Image/CORBIS *page:* 26
© Sergio Dorantes/CORBIS *page:* 29
© Flip Schulke/CORBIS *page:* 29
© David Turnley/CORBIS *page:* 29

Some words are shown in bold, **like this.** You can find what they mean by looking in the glossary.

Contents

"You cannot shake hands with a clenched fist."

—Indira Gandhi

Conflict is a disagreement or struggle between people. When conflict is not handled properly, things can get out of control. Name-calling and harsh words can lead to hurt feelings and grudges that last a long time. In the worst situations, conflict can lead to violence.

Conflict does not have to be negative. When people sit down together and talk about their problems, they make the world a more peaceful place. They show others that violence is not the only way to handle disputes.

Conflict resolution is the process of working with others to peacefully solve problems. Conflict resolution means searching for nonviolent solutions. In the process, we can learn about others and ourselves.

Stopping the violence

Maya rushes through the hall with an armload of books. If she does not hurry, she will be late for class. As she turns the corner toward her classroom, she slams into Shani. Shani's books scatter across the hallway.

Shani puts her hands on her hips and glares at Maya. She says, "Maya, you're such a loser! You're not the only one who's late for class."

Maya is angry that Shani called her a loser. But as she looks at the other girl's clenched fists and tense expression, Maya knows what to do. She says, "I'm sorry, Shani. Let me help you pick up your books."

Shani sees Maya's apologetic expression, and her face softens and her fists unclench. "I'm sorry I called you a loser," she says to Maya. "I'm having a really bad day."

Conflict does not have to be hurtful or violent.

The Key Is Keeping Calm

Everyone gets angry. Anger is a normal emotion and a part of life. Nearly every day you will come across something that might make you mad. Being angry can even be positive. It can prompt people to change things in life that are unfair.

You cannot erase anger from your life. But you can learn how to express and handle angry feelings. The most important thing to remember is to stay calm. Try putting your feelings into words. You might say, for example, "I am really mad at Jenna because she ignored me in math class." Once you have identified whom you are angry with, and why, then you can begin to think of peaceful ways to solve your problem.

Keeping Your Cool

- Take a deep breath.
- Count to ten before you speak.
- Walk away until you feel calmer.
- Talk about your feelings.

The Guardian Angels run programs to help people learn how to become mediators and resolve conflicts peacefully.

When tempers flare, it is not always easy to keep cool. That is where **mediators** are most helpful. Mediators are people who help others work out their problems. A key role of the mediator is to make sure people stay calm.

Accepting a person's culture and heritage is an important part of respect.

N o two people are alike. Some like reading while others enjoy watching football on television. Some people have dark skin while others have light skin. People's differences make the world a more interesting place.

To be a good problem solver, you must **respect** other people. Respect means being able to accept others for who they are. It means not judging people based on their race, religion, or capability. It means allowing people to have their own thoughts and opinions.

Sometimes people judge others before getting to know them. This is called **prejudice.** Prejudice is unfair, and it can cause conflict. It is important to remember that people are more alike than different and to treat others as your equals.

Rebecca Payne is a person who has been hurt by prejudice. At her high school in Oregon, Rebecca was harassed and called names because of her Native American heritage. At first, Rebecca was hurt and angry. Then she decided to do something about her feelings.

Rebecca and her family started a Native American dance group that performed at high schools and other places throughout the state. After performing their dances, the group talked to the audience about Native American culture. Rebecca showed others how proud she was of her ancestry. She was able to teach her fellow students about her culture and explain why she did some things differently. Once the other students learned about the history of Rebecca's people, they became respectful and wanted to learn more.

These campers join together from across the United States. Background differences do not stop them from having fun.

Every story has more than one side. Each person who tells the tale sees it differently. The same holds true for arguments and disagreements. Each person sees the conflict from a different point of view. It is important to consider all sides of the conflict before jumping to a conclusion.

Do you want to settle a dispute with your friend Jim? Take a minute to think about the problem from his point of view. What is his opinion of the conflict? Remember to focus on Jim's feelings. He probably feels hurt and angry, just like you.

Ben Smilowitz believes that kids everywhere have the right to express their points of view.

Once you have both talked about your feelings, then talk about the issue itself. It is okay for you to disagree with your friend. But do so respectfully. Remember that he also has a right to his feelings and thoughts. Do not try to place blame or decide who is "right" and who is "wrong."

Former Vermont governor Howard Dean signs a bill to create a seat for students on the state's Board of Education.

Connecticut resident Ben Smilowitz believes that kids everywhere should be allowed to speak out about issues that affect them. Because all students are affected by school rules and policies, Ben thinks they have the right to share their points of view. So when Ben was in high school, he took action.

Ben wrote a **bill** that created two special seats for students on the state's board of education. The board of education writes rules and regulations for all of the state's schools. Ben worked hard to get his bill passed, and in 1998 the bill became a law. Connecticut students now have a say in making important education decisions. Allowing people who are affected by specific laws to have a voice in creating those laws can deter conflict and resolve outstanding issues.

Today Ben is older, but he still cares about what kids have to say. He continues to work so young people around the country can share their thoughts and feelings about important issues.

Communication is an important tool to resolve differences. Nothing will be settled if you stop talking. Grudges will continue, anger will grow, and friendships will be lost.

People who are good problem-solvers know that they must be good listeners first. Before you can work on fixing a bad situation, you must understand the problem. This means listening to what others have to say.

Another key part of communicating is talking to others about your thoughts and feelings. This is especially important when something is bothering you. Talking

How to Be a Good Listener

- Look the speaker in the eye.
- Do not interrupt.
- Nod your head to let the speaker know you are listening.
- Do not offer advice or pass judgment.
- If the speaker is unclear, ask questions.

With the help of a mentor, teens in Los Angeles
staff a teen help line. Teens can call the help line
and talk about their problems and feelings.

about your problems allows people who care about you
to help.

When you are telling a friend about something that
has upset you, here are some helpful hints.

- Use "I" messages. Do not say, "You should not have
  done that." Instead try, "I feel angry when you borrow
  my shirt without asking."

- Keep calm. Yelling or talking loudly is not the way to get
  your message across.

- Look the other person in the eye.

For decades, African Americans were not treated equally in the United States. In some parts of the country, blacks were separated, or **segregated,** from whites. African-American children had to go to separate schools and drink from separate water fountains. Black people had to sit apart from white people in movie theaters, on buses, and at restaurants.

In 1960 four young African-American men decided to use nonviolence to change their world. On a February afternoon, the four entered a department store in

An African-American college student sits at a "whites-only" lunch counter in Birmingham, Alabama, to protest segregation.

In 1955 Rosa Parks refused to give up her seat on a Montgomery, Alabama, bus to a white man. Her act of nonviolent protest led to a law that banned segregation on Montgomery buses.

Greensboro, North Carolina. Although the teens knew that the lunch counter in the store was for whites only, they sat down and ordered coffee, doughnuts, and soda. The waiter refused to serve them, but the four men sat quietly until the lunch counter closed.

Over the next few months, the number of protests grew. By April people in 54 U.S. cities held their own sit-ins at whites-only restaurants.

The nonviolent protests worked. Six months after the first sit-in, the four teens who had started it all returned to the Greensboro store and were served. The sit-ins focused attention on racism in the United States. They helped end segregation and make the country a more equal place for all.

Many kids say that bullying is one of the biggest problems in schools today. **Bullying** is any act of physical, verbal, or emotional violence that is meant to hurt someone. Pinching, shoving, hair-pulling, and name-calling are just a few of the ways that bullies can make someone's life miserable. Leaving someone out from group activities or spreading gossip about them is also bullying behavior.

How to Handle a Bully

Here are some tips that might help if a bully bothers you.

- Talk to an adult about the bullying. Ask that person for help.
- Never use violence when dealing with a bully. Violence will only make the situation worse.
- Walk away from the bully.
- Ignore the bully.
- Try to stay with friends when the bully is around. Most bullies will not pick on someone who is with a group.

If you have ever been a bully's victim, then you know bullying hurts. Being pushed around and teased makes a person feel bad. It robs a person of **self-respect.** Being bullied can cause you to have nightmares, illness, and poor grades. It can also lead to violence and physical harm.

Bullying of any type is wrong. Nobody deserves to be picked on. If you see someone being bullied, you can help. Let bullies know you do not agree with their behavior. If the bullying persists, report it to an adult.

Bullying can lead to violence and physical harm. If you see someone being bullied, tell an adult.

Everyone deserves to attend a school that is safe and secure. Some kids are working on ways to make sure their schools are peaceful places to learn. In Elk Grove, California, high school students decided to put an end to bullying and violence in their school. They formed a

In 1999 Craig Scott's sister was killed by another student at Columbine High School in Colorado. After the tragedy, Craig traveled around the country, talking to students about peace and nonviolence.

Erika Harold, Miss America 2003, speaks out against bullying and violence in schools.

group called Teens for Tolerance. The group meets each month to discuss ways to stop harassment and bullying. The group members also help other kids learn how to respect each other's differences.

In 1989 Alex Orange, an eighteen-year-old high school student, was shot to death in North Carolina. The young man died trying to stop a fight at a party. His classmates were outraged and horrified. They wanted to make sure this never happened again. A student and a teacher formed a group called S.A.V.E.—Students Against Violence Everywhere. The organization helps young people learn how to handle conflict and avoid violence.

Today, S.A.V.E. is going strong and growing. Students in 35 different states have started their own groups. More than 93,000 students have signed up to help stop violence.

Members of rival gangs in Providence, Rhode Island, work out their conflicts on the football field instead of on the streets.

Everybody makes mistakes. Part of **conflict resolution** is accepting responsibility for your actions. If you have made a mistake, admit it to yourself and to others.

When you wrong a friend or family member, you should apologize. When you say, "I am sorry," people learn to **respect** you. They realize you are a strong person who is not afraid to own up to mistakes.

Sometimes you may be the one who is hurt. In some cases you may never get an apology from a person who hurt you. Other people, however, might be brave enough to admit that they were wrong. They might ask you to forgive them.

When people sincerely apologize to you, it is important to try to forgive them. Forgiving can be very difficult, especially when you have been badly hurt. It may take some time to forgive. But in the end, it is worth the effort. Forgiving others helps break the cycle of violence and hatred.

One person who learned about the power of forgiving was Nickole Evans. When she was fourteen years old, two teenage boys attacked Nickole and her friend. The boys shot at the two girls with BB guns. The small pellets hit Nickole's side and her friend's head.

Although unharmed after the attack, Nickole was frightened and angry. In time Nickole chose to forgive the boys. Since then she has become an activist for nonviolence and peace. Trained as a **peer mediator,** Nickole helps students in her school peacefully resolve conflict. She has even started a chapter of S.A.V.E. in her school.

Teens from countries in conflict get to know one another at the Seeds of Peace camp in Otisfield, Maine. Here, they learn that respect, tolerance, and forgiveness are important to world peace.

Dontale King (left), Malik Generett, Tyrone Foreman, and Kieshawn Smallwood, participate in Freedom Schools, a summer program that teaches conflict resolution skills and open-mindedness.

Fairness is an important part of conflict resolution. Being fair means finding a solution that everyone thinks is reasonable and honest. If the solution to a problem is not fair, one person may feel angry and hurt. New problems may occur later. A person who is not treated fairly will be less likely to take part in peaceful problem solving again.

Resolving conflict is not about figuring out who is right and who is wrong. It is about **compromise.** In a compromise you willingly give up something in order to resolve a problem. The other person also gives up

Thurgood Marshall

 Thurgood Marshall found out firsthand about racism and **prejudice.** In 1929 Marshall was not allowed to attend a law school in Maryland because he was black. The young man did not give up, however. He attended a university for African Americans and earned his law degree there. For the rest of his life, Marshall used his knowledge to challenge laws in the United States that were unfair to blacks. In 1967 he was appointed to the U.S. Supreme Court, the first African American to earn that honor. Until his death in 1993, Marshall continued fighting for the civil rights of all Americans.

something. In return, you can both feel good about working together to solve your problem.

The next time you and a friend disagree, try compromising. First, brainstorm a number of ways to handle the problem. Then sit down together and share your ideas. Together you can find a solution that works for both of you.

If you get stuck, do not be afraid to ask a trusted friend or adult for help. Sometimes a third party can help you see when a compromise is fair or unfair.

Do you use good conflict resolution skills when you have a problem with a parent?

It is easy to talk about fixing something that is wrong, but actually doing it is more difficult. Read the following examples of conflict. Before reading the suggested solutions, brainstorm ways that you might solve each problem. Remember that the solution should be fair to everyone involved.

Jarrell dislikes his new stepfather. Paul bosses him around all the time. And Paul is always suggesting that they toss around a football or play a game of chess together. Jarrell does not like those activities. Life was a lot easier when his own dad was around.

Jarrell has a few ways to solve his problem. He could ask for a family meeting where everyone can talk about their feelings. He can tell his stepdad that he does not like football or chess, and offer to do something different together. Jarrell can also talk to a guidance counselor, teacher, or another trusted adult about his feelings.

Kelli is talking on the phone with Megan. Megan wants help with her science homework again. Kelli knows that Megan really needs her help, but she does not care. The only time that Megan talks to her is after school, when she wants something. At school Megan ignores Kelli and acts like she does not even know her. As she listens to Megan's pleading voice, Kelli becomes angry.

Kelli feels hurt and angry about the way Megan treats her at school. She can be courageous and talk to Megan about her hurt feelings. Kelli can also call Megan back after talking to a parent or another friend about the problem.

Talking to Parents and Other Adults

It can be hard talking to grown-ups. Sometimes, you may wonder if they really understand what you are feeling. Here are some tips to help you communicate.

- Set aside a block of time so that you and the adult can talk without being distracted.

- Ask the adult to let you talk for up to three minutes without interruption. Allow him or her the same amount of time to talk when you are done.

- Listen to what the adult has to say. Try not to interrupt, overreact, or become upset. Remember that grown-ups have opinions, too.

Some people are professional problem solvers. They use their **conflict resolution** skills every day. In their work they help keep people calm and try to find peaceful solutions to problems in the world.

- *Community mediators* help community members in conflict peacefully resolve their problems. These specially trained professionals work with families, neighbors, and other groups to find solutions that work for everyone. An example of a community mediator is someone who works in your school as a guidance counselor or social

High school students take part in a model United Nations program. Here, the students learn what it is like to resolve international conflicts and practice diplomacy.

*French United Nations Peacekeepers talk to
a U.S. Air Force pilot on the airfield.*

worker. Often, these people act as the go-between for
parents, students, and teachers, teaching them how to
positively communicate with each other.

- *United Nations (UN) peacekeepers* are people who put
  their lives on the line for world peace. UN peacekeepers
  travel to countries in conflict, like Iraq, Afghanistan, or
  Bosnia. They work to keep the peace in these nations.

- *Ambassadors* are people who represent their country
  in a foreign land. The United States has ambassadors in
  many different nations around the world. These
  ambassadors make sure that relations between the
  United States and other nations are in good shape.
  Sometimes an ambassador must try to solve problems
  that arise between the two countries.

Former President Jimmy Carter shakes hands with Palestinian leader Yasser Arafat. Carter still works hard to spread world peace.

In 1977 Georgia politician James Earl Carter Jr. became the 39th president of the United States. As the nation's leader, "Jimmy" Carter made world peace one of his top causes. During his four years in office, he encouraged other world leaders to work out their differences without resorting to violence or bloodshed. He helped negotiate a number of peace treaties in different parts of the world.

Since he left the White House in 1981, Carter has kept busy promoting peace. The following year he founded the Carter Center in Atlanta, Georgia. People from around the world come to the Carter Center to learn how to resolve conflicts and work for world peace.

Carter also practices what he preaches. The former president travels to countries that are fighting or on the brink of war. He spreads the message that peace is the only answer to today's international issues. In 2002 Carter was awarded the Nobel Peace Prize for his "decades of untiring effort to find peaceful solutions to international conflicts."

The Nobel Peace Prize

Since 1901 this special award has been given to a person or people who work hard to spread the message: Peace is the answer. Past winners include Martin Luther King Jr., Nelson Mandela, and Mother Teresa of Calcutta. To learn more about this special prize, check out the Nobel e-Museum at www.nobel.se.

Nelson Mandela

Reverend Martin
Luther King Jr.

Mother Teresa

*These three Nobel Peace Prize winners
worked tirelessly for world peace.*

Glossary

bill first draft of a law

bullying using physical, verbal, or emotional violence to hurt someone

compromise working out a problem by having all sides give up something

conflict resolution process of working with others to peacefully solve problems

mediator person who helps others work out their problems

peer mediator a student who is trained to help other students work out their problems and conflicts

prejudice judging others before getting to know them

respect accepting other people as they are

segregation legal separation of people based on race

self-respect the feeling that you have pride in your values, your decisions, and your actions

Garrison, Jennifer, and Andrew Tubesing, editors. *A Million Visions of Peace: Wisdom from the Friends of Old Turtle.* Duluth, Minn.: Pfeifer-Hamilton Publications, 2001.
In this book, children's messages of peace are combined with bright, colorful illustrations.

Johnston, Marianne. *Dealing with Anger: The Conflict Resolution Library.* New York: Hazelden/Powerkids Press, 1999.
This book contains a discussion of anger and includes helpful hints on how to deal with this strong emotion.

Lalli, Judy. *Make Someone Smile: And Forty More Ways to Be a Peacemaker.* Minneapolis: Free Spirit Publishing, 1996.
This book contains suggestions on how to handle conflict and be a peacemaker.

Moser, Adolph. *Don't Rant and Rave on Wednesdays.* Kansas City, Mo.: Landmark Editions, 1994.
This work contains tips and tricks to help kids control their anger.

Index